ME TOO!® BOOKS

NOBODY KNEW BUT GOD!

MIRIAM AND BABY MOSES

By Marilyn Lashbrook

Illustrated by Stephanie McFetridge Britt

RAINBOW
STUDIES
INTERNATIONAL

El Reno, Oklahoma

Creating Colorful Treasures™

ME TOO! ® Books are designed to help you share the joy of reading with children. They provide a new and fun way to improve a child's reading skills — by practice and example. At the same time, you are teaching your children valuable Bible truths.

Little children can play a big part in God's plan. NOBODY KNEW BUT GOD! will help children realize the importance of fulfilling their responsibilities. They will also be reminded that when they are going through tough times, God has not forgotten them. He is working out His plan day by day. This story will present you with an opportunity to discuss with your child ways she or he can help your family...through words, actions and prayers.

Reading is the key to successful education. Obeying the principles of God's Word opens the door to a successful life. **ME TOO!**® Books encourage your children in both!

Bold type:	Child reads.
Regular type:	Adult reads.

⬣ Wait for child to respond.

❤❤ Talk about it!

Library of Congress Catalog Card Number: 98-065498
ISBN 0-933657-86-2

Art direction and design by Chris Schechner Graphic Design.
Production and film by Paragon Communications Group, Inc.

1 2 3 4 5 6 7 8 9 — 02 01 00 99 98
Rainbow Studies International, El Reno, OK 73036, U.S.A.

Nobody Knew But God!

MIRIAM AND BABY MOSES

Taken from Exodus 1-2 and Hebrews 11:23

Long ago in a land of great wonders, lived a Hebrew girl named Miriam. Egypt was filled with Hebrew people. But they were not welcome there. The Egyptians made life hard for them.

Pharaoh the Egyptian King was worried. "There are too many Hebrews," he said to his people, "and they are more mighty than we are."

"What if there is a war?" he asked. "The Hebrew people may fight us!"

So Pharaoh put slave drivers over the Hebrews and forced them to do backbreaking work.

Pharaoh didn't know it . . . but the harder he made the Hebrews work, the stronger they grew. And God blessed His people with more and more children.

When Pharaoh saw the slaves were having even more children, he devised a terrible plan. He commanded the people, "Every boy baby that is born must be thrown into the Nile River."

Pharaoh didn't know it . . . but this would fit right into God's plan. And God had a big plan!

Things looked bad, but God had not forgotten His people.

One day Miriam heard a secret. Her mother was going to have a baby. Miriam was going to be a big sister.

Planning for a baby is exciting. There are names to choose, clothes to make, a cradle to prepare, and daydreams to dream of holding a tiny newborn baby.

Lullaby in Egypt land,

Pyramids and desert sand.

Lullaby soft and true,

God has not forgotten you.

When it was time, Miriam's mother had her baby. It was a handsome boy. A boy! Now what would they do? Surely they couldn't throw this tiny baby into the river!

Miriam's parents had faith in God. They wouldn't let fear stop them from doing what was right. They believed God wanted this baby to live.

For three months they hid the baby. But as he grew, it was harder and harder to hide him. When babies get older they get bigger and noisier, and they stay awake longer.

What do you do to keep a baby quiet?
You walk him, and rock him, and feed him,
and burp him, and change him, and jiggle
him, and play with him, and sing to him.
Being a big sister or brother is a lot
of work!

One day Miriam's mother knew she could not hide the baby in her house any longer. She must take him some place safe.

She took a sturdy basket and coated it inside and outside with tar. The tar filled in the cracks. When it was dry, the basket was watertight. It would not leak.

Miriam's mother gently placed the baby into the basket and covered him. Then she and Miriam took him to the river.

They placed the basket in the water. Reeds and river grasses kept it from floating away.

Then the baby's mother did something very hard for a mother to do. She turned and walked away from her baby.

With her heart breaking, Miriam's mother went home. She ached to hold her dear baby. But she had to leave him in order to save his life.

She didn't know it . . . but she would have her son back soon.

Miriam did not go home. She stayed to see what would happen. It must have taken a lot of courage to stay by herself. But her baby brother's life might depend on her.

Miriam waited and watched. Then she heard something. Someone was coming. Miriam looked up.

She saw a young woman dressed in beautiful clothes. Golden jewelry sparkled in the woman's dark hair. It was the princess!

The princess! Pharaoh's daughter! Pharaoh had made the law about killing baby boys.

What if the princess found the baby? Would she obey her father's law? Would she have the baby killed?

The princess was bathing in the river when she saw the little boat floating among the river grasses. She called to her maidens, "Bring the little boat to me."

Her servant girls went to get the basket-boat. They brought it to the princess.

The princess opened the basket. The baby cried. Poor baby!

"This is one of the Hebrew children,"
said the princess. Her heart went out to the
tiny, frightened child.

Miriam came closer. With her heart pounding, she asked the princess, "Would you like for me to find a Hebrew nurse to take care of the baby for you?"

"Go," said Pharaoh's daughter.

Miriam went. She ran as fast as she could. She ran to find her mother.

When they returned, the princess said to Miriam's mother, "Take this baby and nurse it for me. I will pay you."

So Miriam and her mother went home. They were glad to be taking the baby back, too.

Miriam's courage may have saved the baby's life. Miriam didn't know it . . . but one day, the baby would grow up and save her life.

When the baby was old enough, he went to live with the princess. He became her adopted son.

"I will name him Moses," she said, "because I drew him out of the water." The princess didn't know it . . . but one day, God would use Moses to draw His people out of Egypt.

Pharaoh didn't know his evil plans would help God's people.

But God knew.

Pharaoh's daughter didn't know the name she chose for the baby foretold God's plan for him.

But God knew.

Miriam's parents didn't know that all the problems they faced would be for the good of their people.

But God knew.

Miriam didn't know she would be a big part of God's plan.

But God knew.

Lullaby, do not fear,

Wipe away that tear.

Things look bad, but it's still true,

God has not forgotten you.

ME TOO!®
B O O K S

Ages 2-7

SOMEONE TO LOVE
THE STORY OF CREATION

TWO BY TWO
THE STORY OF NOAH'S FAITH

I DON'T WANT TO
THE STORY OF JONAH

I MAY BE LITTLE
THE STORY OF DAVID'S GROWTH

I'LL PRAY ANYWAY
THE STORY OF DANIEL

WHO NEEDS A BOAT?
THE STORY OF MOSES

GET LOST, LITTLE BROTHER
THE STORY OF JOSEPH

THE WALL THAT DID NOT FALL
THE STORY OF RAHAB'S FAITH

NO TREE FOR CHRISTMAS
THE STORY OF JESUS' BIRTH

NOW I SEE
THE STORY OF THE MAN BORN BLINI

DON'T ROCK THE BOAT!
THE STORY OF THE MIRACULOUS CAT(

OUT ON A LIMB
THE STORY OF ZACCHAEUS

SOWING AND GROWING
THE PARABLE OF THE SOWER AND THE S

DON'T STOP. . . FILL EVERY PO
THE STORY OF THE WIDOW'S OIL

GOOD, BETTER, BEST
THE STORY OF MARY AND MARTHA

GOD'S HAPPY HELPERS
THE STORY OF TABITHA AND FRIEND

Ages 5-10

IT'S NOT MY FAULT
MAN'S BIG MISTAKE

GOD, PLEASE SEND FIRE!
ELIJAH AND THE
PROPHETS OF BAAL

TOO BAD, AHAB
NABOTH'S VINEYARD

THE WEAK STRONGMAN
SAMSON

NOTHING TO FEAR
JESUS WALKS ON WATER

THE BEST DAY EVER
THE STORY OF JESUS

THE GREAT SHAKE-UP
MIRACLES IN PHILIPPI

TWO LADS AND A DAD
THE PRODIGAL SON

NOBODY KNEW BUT G(
MIRIAM AND BABY MOSE**S**

MORE THAN BEAUTIFU
THE STORY OF ESTHER

FAITH TO FIGHT
THE STORY OF CALEB

BIG ENEMY, BIGGER G(
THE STORY OF GIDEON

WE SEE!™
V I D E O S

VIDEOS FOR TODAY'S CHRISTIAN FAMILY.
51 animated Bible stories from the Old Testament ("In the Beginning" Series) and New Testament ("A Kingdom without Frontiers" Series) will provide your children with a solid cornerstone of spiritual support.

Available at your local bookstore or from:
Rainbow Studies International
P.O. Box 759 • El Reno, Oklahoma 73036 • 1-800-242-5348

RSI
Creating Colorful Treas